SITTIN' ON THE PATIO

31 Daily Poetic Devotions to Renew Your Spirit

A beautiful collection of daily devotions, uniquely written
to renew your soul and lift your spirit.

Pat Stahl

bush
PUBLISHING
& associates

Unless otherwise indicated, all Scripture quotations are taken from the New King James Version of the Bible, copyright © 1979, 1980, 1982, Thomas Nelson, Inc., Publishers.

All Scripture quotations marked KJV are taken from the King James Version of the Bible.

SITTIN' ON THE PATIO

31 Daily Poetic Devotions to Renew Your Spirit

A beautiful collection of daily devotions, uniquely written to renew your soul and lift your spirit.

Copyright © 2025 Pat Stahl SITTIN' ON THE PATIO

ISBN Print: 978-1-944566-82-1

Bush Publishing & Associates, LLC books are available at major retailers and on Amazon.com.

For further information, please contact:

Bush Publishing & Associates

Tulsa, Oklahoma

www.bushpublishing.com

Printed in the United States of America.

No portion of this book may be used or reproduced by any means: graphic, electronic or mechanical, including photocopying, recording, taping, or by any information storage retrieval system, without the written permission of the publisher, except in the case of brief quotations embodied in critical articles and reviews.

DEDICATION

This book is dedicated to the glory of God for His love and teachings; to my church, family, and friends for being such a big part in my life, and to all who will read this book and be blessed.

FOREWARD

What a special privilege it is to introduce this beautiful collection of daily devotions, uniquely written from the heart of one of God's faithful servants. In these pages, you will discover more than poetry—you will hear a lifetime of faith, prayer, and devotion poured into words that encourage, comfort, and inspire.

Each poem is a gentle reminder of God's presence in our everyday lives. Whether rejoicing in His blessings or leaning on His strength in times of trial, these verses invite you to draw closer to the Lord and see His hand at work in all things.

I pray these devotions will bless you as much as Pat's life and words have blessed me and so many others.

Pastor Trey Waller

Pastor Trey Waller

Living Word Minden

Minden, Louisiana

ACKNOWLEDGMENTS

Thanks be to God, who through His Holy Spirit gave me the messages for this book.

My heartfelt thanks to my pastors—David and Paige Divelbiss, Andy and Jemmie Maddox, Trey and Kelli Waller and Jeff and Sherry Scott—who have taught, nurtured, and encouraged me over the past 20 years.

Special thanks to Wayne Orr, a dear friend and English teacher, for his help with the wording of the book. And to my best friend, Trudy Bishop, and my family, thank you for being my faithful "sounding boards" and constant support.

TABLE OF CONTENTS

Day One 15

Day Two 21

Day Three 27

Day Four 33

Day Five 37

Day Six 43

Day Seven 49

Day Eight................................ 55

Day Nine 61

Day Ten 67

Day Eleven 71

Day Twelve............................ 77

Day Thirteen 83

Day Fourteen 89

Day Fifteen 95

Day Sixteen 101

Day Seventeen 105

Day Eighteen 111

Day Nineteen 117

Day Twenty 123

Day Twenty One 129

Day Twenty Two................ 135

Day Twenty Three 139

Day Twenty Four.............. 143

Day Twenty Five 147

Day Twenty Six 153

Day Twenty Seven 159

Day Twenty Eight 165

Day Twenty Nine.............. 169

Day Thirty 175

Day Thirty One................. 179

About The Author 183

DAY ONE

"Entreat me not to leave you, Or to turn back from following after you; For wherever you go, I will go; And wherever you lodge, I will lodge; Your people shall be my people, And your God, my God."

—Ruth 1:16

*I'm sittin' on the patio with my open Bible in my lap.
What do you want to declare this morning, Father, as
into your Word I tap?*

*Your Word that I'm reading is in the book of Ruth.
Perhaps this is where I'll find today's truth.*

*Naomi, Ruth, and Orpah lost their husbands, and their
backs were to the wall. That must have been a hard and
lonely time for them all.*

*Orpah returned to her family, but Ruth, after her
husband died, forsook all, To go with Naomi to her
homeland of Judah to follow her call.*

*When I think of Ruth, those special words—"wherever
you go, I will go"—come to mind. For as she goes with
Naomi, a fulfilled life she will eventually find.*

*When they got to Judah, life didn't get easy over night,
For every day's sustenance was a hard and burdensome
fight.*

Sittin' on the Patio

Ruth's gleaning the corn fields of Boaz behind the reapers hired,

Found favor with Boaz, as she reaped plenty of grain, though very tired.

As she continued to provide for her and Naomi's welfare, A series of events occurred to which none can compare.

Naomi told Ruth to lay at the feet of Boaz as he slept in the night, As he was their nearest kinsman, she would be his wife by right.

She did as was told and arose before any could see. Only Boaz told her there was a nearer kinsman than he.

According to law, Boaz approached this kinsman offering him Ruth, his by inheritance But when the kinsman could not buy her, Boaz now had a chance.

Before the elders and all the people, Boaz declared Ruth his rightfully purchased wife that day, Giving Ruth and Naomi a home where forever they could stay.

A son, Obed, was born to Boaz and Ruth in time, But that certainly wasn't the end of the line.

For through Obed's lineage came King David and

eventually one even greater, The Lord Jesus Christ, our own Lord and Savior.

Ruth was full of love and faithfulness. She met the mark and passed the test.

So, Father, what is your Word saying to me? "Remain obedient, loving, and faithful–and my glory and strength you will surely see."

Life Application:

Ruth and Naomi persevered and received God's best. When things are hard, unsure, and hopeless, just be faithful to God. 2 Chronicles 16:9 says, "The eyes of the Lord run to and fro throughout the whole earth to show Himself strong on behalf of those whose heart is loyal to Him."

Confession:

My born-again heart is perfect toward you, and Lord, I know you see my heart and will show yourself strong on my behalf today.

DAY TWO

"Blessed be the name of God forever and ever, For wisdom and might are His. And He changes the times and the seasons; He removes kings and raises up kings; He gives wisdom to the wise And knowledge to those who have understanding. He reveals deep and secret things; He knows what is in the darkness, And light dwells with Him."

—Daniel 2:20-22

I'm sittin' on the patio for the third time today And with each sitting, I'm gleaning your Word through Daniel; therefore, Father, what do you have to say?

Prophecy comes to mind when over the book of Daniel I ponder, But to the lion's den and fiery furnace my mind begins to wander.

Daniel and his three friends were called by King Nebuchadnezzar to serve him and be his own, Even given new names by which they were known.

Daniel and his friends ate not of the King's menu while there, And grew stronger than those who did the King's delicacies share.

God gave them knowledge and wisdom in all things, it seems, And to Daniel, special understanding of visions and dreams.

The King had a troubling dream which he could not

remember, And for those who could not interpret it, the King gave a decree to dismember.

But Daniel asked God to reveal the King's dream to him, And God blessed Daniel with the vision he did send.

Daniel interpreted the dream, and the King acknowledged Daniel's God that day. He was pleased with Daniel and promoted him, as well as his three friends, by the way.

Now King Nebuchadnezzar made a golden statue of himself to which all were to bow down. However, Shadrach, Meshack, and Abednego would not bow; word got around.

At the fury of the King, they were thrown into the fiery furnace to burn. In their midst was a fourth man, Jesus, whom even the King did discern.

Calling them forth there wasn't a single hair that was singed on their heads. They didn't even smell of smoke when they should have been dead.

The King promoted them further and made a new decree, That their God could be worshipped and

PAT STAHL

honored from bended knee.

The King had another dream whose interpretation would be his demise, Until he lifted up his head in praise to the God in the skies.

Later on, a new King Belshazzar defiled the temple's vessels when a party to the Gods was thrown. Handwriting on the wall appeared–its message unknown.

Daniel was called to interpret, but the word was not good. That very night, the King's end came quickly as the message said it would.

At Belshazzar's death, a new King, Darius, came to the throne. Once again, all were supposed to pray and bow to King Darius, but since Daniel would not bow, into the lions' den he was thrown.

King Darius liked Daniel, and to the King's delight, an angel of God came and shut the mouths of the lions that night. Daniel was brought up from the den while his accusers were cast in–what a terrible sight.

Daniel himself had many dreams and visions, as for his people he prayed; Much was revealed to him by the ancient of days.

Sittin' on the Patio

So Lord, from your Word regarding Daniel and his friends, obedience and faithfulness one can learn. From their actions, we, too, this truth can discern.

Life Application:

Daniel and his three friends were faithful to God not only in the good times but also when times were bad. In fact, in the very worst of times, we recall Joshua 1:5 where God said to Joshua, "No man shall be able to stand before you all the days of your life; as I was with Moses, so I will be with you. I will not leave you nor forsake you."

Confession:

I will not fear what may come my way because I know, Lord, you are right here with me now and always to protect and defend.

DAY THREE

"Stand therefore, having girded your waist with truth, having put on the breastplate of righteousness, and having shod your feet with the preparation of the gospel of peace; above all, taking the shield of faith with which you will be able to quench all the fiery darts of the wicked one. And take the helmet of salvation, and the sword of the Spirit, which is the word of God; praying always with all prayer and supplication in the Spirit, being watchful to this end with all perseverance and supplication for all the saints—and for me, that utterance may be given to me, that I may open my mouth boldly to make known the mystery of the gospel..."

—EPHESIANS 6:14-19

I'm sittin' on the patio in the cool of a summer morn, What do you have to reveal, Father? What new revelation today is born?

Your Word that I'm reading is Ephesians chapter six today. I know it's about your armour and fighting the fight of faith your way.

But before the armour, you talk about the family, And certain duties for each of them is plain to see.

Children are admonished to obey their parents, for it is right. Here, long life is promised to those who keep that in sight.

Fathers are supposed to nurture their own children–not to provoke, Bringing them up in your instruction, being careful their spirits not to choke.

Servants are to serve with obedience and from the heart, Serving as unto the Lord as they fulfill their part.

Sittin' on the Patio

Masters are to treat their servants the same as their master in heaven, Being careful of their hearts as their orders are given.

How can we be the persons the Lord wants us to be, As we stand against the wiles of the devil, even in places we cannot see?

We can put on your whole armour from head to toe, Praying always in the spirit wherever we may go.

You are saying as I look into your Word as well as into your face, To live, not unto men, but unto you and to receive your peace and grace.

Life Application:

God has given us instructions for every circumstance in life. He knows what is best for us and what will lead us to a fulfilled life. Proverbs 3:5 says, "Trust in the Lord with all your heart, and lean not on your own understanding; in all your ways acknowledge Him, and he will direct your paths."

Confession:

Through the Holy Spirit, who is my helper, I will hear, receive, and walk in your ways, Father, trusting you with my whole heart.

DAY FOUR

"Finally, brethren, whatever things are true, whatever things are noble, whatever things are just, whatever things are pure, whatever things are lovely, whatever things are of good report, if there is any virtue and if there is anything praiseworthy—meditate on these things."

—Philippians 4:8

I'm sittin' on the patio listening to the early morning sounds. What do you have to say today, Lord? What can you expound?

Your Word is open to Philippians chapter four Paul is exhorting believers to live for you more.

Paul's early life was filled with living in the flesh and following the law. Before he knew Jesus, on his own abilities and knowledge, he did draw.

But when he met Jesus, his life took on a new direction, Seeking not his own but Jesus' knowledge and perfection.

All that he had done and attained, much it was indeed; He counted all as loss, for direction now from Jesus he did heed.

The righteousness Paul had found in keeping the law by jot and by tittle, Was nothing compared to

Sittin' on the Patio

righteousness by faith in Jesus–the former mattered little.

Paul had to forget all that was in the past and reach ahead, Making his goal the high calling of God in Christ Jesus instead.

Paul exhorts believers to follow his example as their walk in faith does unfold, To be of one mind and purpose to make Jesus above all their ultimate goal.

Life Application:

Paul had great zeal in all he did, both in following the law and then in following Jesus. God used that zeal to reach many to come to believe in Jesus and receive Him as their savior. Romans 12:11 "Not lagging in diligence, fervent in spirit, serving the Lord."

Confession:

I will be zealous for you, Jesus, to receive more of you and to give more of you to others.

DAY FIVE

"Come to me, all you who labor and are heavy laden, and I will give you rest. Take my yoke upon you and learn from me, for I am gentle and lowly in heart, and you will find rest for your souls. For my yoke is easy and my burden is light."

—Matthew 11:28-30

Pat Stahl

I'm sittin' on the patio–the morning sun is casting shadows on each tree. What do you have to say today, Lord? What do you want me to see?

Your Word on my lap is opened to 2 Corinthians chapter eleven, Paul is warning of those who come in and spoil the leaven.

The devil appears many times as an angel of light, Twisting and complicating truth that was simple and right.

Paul had a Godly jealousy for the people he established in the faith to believe, And warned them to be careful of those who would corrupt and deceive.

Paul had been the chiefest of sinners before he met Jesus, But since his conversion, his faith had become one of trust.

More than most were the trials and tests he endured,

SITTIN' ON THE PATIO

But coming through them, his faith was even more assured.

He knew down deep in his heart that Jesus was his all in all, And, though knocked down, he knew that in trusting Him, he would never fall.

Moreover, Father, today's Word may be a little difficult to swallow, Realizing that sufferings may come as your Son, we follow.

But there is nothing that man can do to any child of yours, That would ever separate them from your love– of that we are assured.

Lord, we trust in you with all our heart and soul, Knowing that whatever the devil dishes out, we are safe in your arms to hold.

Life Application:

Life may take many twists and turns as we tread along. There may be some hard knocks and seemingly unbearable burdens to bear. But you are always with us, for Matthew 11:28-30 reads, "Come to me, all you who labor and are heavy laden, and I will give you rest. Take my yoke upon you and learn from me, for I am gentle and lowly in heart, and you will find rest for your souls. For my yoke is easy and my burden is light."

Confession:

I cast my burdens on you, Lord, for you to carry for me; I give you thanks.

DAY SIX

"For if you remain completely silent at this time, relief and deliverance will arise for the Jews from another place, but you and your father's house will perish. Yet who knows whether you have come to the kingdom for such a time as this?"

—Esther 4:14

I'm sittin' on the patio watching a little bird build her nest. Each day it gets more complete, and in it soon she will rest.

Your Word is open to the book of Esther, as I came to enjoy your voice inside. Henceforth, Father, what do you have to say–what revelation can be my guide?

Esther, just a simple Jewish girl, though fair and beautiful to see, Was reared by her cousin Mordecai, who took her as his own daughter to be.

As time passed, Queen Vashti displeased the King by disobeying his command, And a decree was given that she no more could come before his extended hand.

A search was begun for a new queen among the fair maidens of the land. Esther was taken before the King, and in time she did stand.

The King loved Esther above all, and she found favor

Sittin' on the Patio

and grace. She became the new Queen in this strange and foreign place.

She kept a secret that her own people were the Jews, For Mordecai had told her not to reveal this damaging news.

However, the time came when her people were about to be killed by decree of the King, And Mordecai advised her she could help to stop this terrible thing.

Could she have been put in the position of Queen for a reason? For such a time as this? Was this her appointed season?

Esther and her people began to fast for three days, As she prepared to approach the King–a thing never dared in those days.

She approached the King, even though she was putting her life on the line. He received her, and then she extended her bold invitation for the King and Haman to dine.

Haman was the villain behind the decree to kill the Jews; in effect, now, Because Mordecai had refused in his presence to bow.

In fact, Haman had built a gallow 50 cubits high to hang Mordecai. His heartfelt wish was that this unyielding Jew would die.

After the banquet, Haman was filled with great pride, But during the King's sleepless night, he found a revelation inside.

Mordecai had saved Haman's life, and the king had not known. Thus, Haman was ordered to proclaim and honor Mordecai in the town.

At the second banquet, Queen Esther told the King, Of the wicked Haman and his decree–a terrible thing.

The King had Haman hanged on the gallow Haman himself did design. And reversed the decree so that all the Jews would be fine.

Moreover, the 10 sons of Haman–enemies of the Jews– were slain, And Mordecai, the Jew, was to sit next to the King–it was proclaimed.

What are you saying about this story so full of power? Could this be the time to stand up for you–could this be the very hour?

Life Application:

Occasionally, the time comes when we must stand up for what we believe, no matter what the circumstances may be. We may not feel safe and secure as we face someone who does not believe as we do. But we remember 2 Timothy 1:7 "For God has not given us a spirit of fear, but of power and of love and of a sound mind."

Confession:

Use me, Lord, to speak for you, for I trust in you and love you.

DAY SEVEN

"Examine me, O Lord, and prove me; try my mind and my heart, for your lovingkindness is before my eyes, and I have walked in your truth."

—P<small>SALM</small> 26:2-3

I'm sittin' on the patio thanking God for who He is and for all He has done, Resting in his creation and his blessings at the rising of the sun.

Your Word on my lap is open to Isaiah chapter fifty-eight. What do you have to express, Lord? All of your Word is great!

You speak of the fast observed according to your will and your way, That it is much more than abstaining from nourishment for the day.

The fast is not the things that are there for the world to see, Like sackcloth and ashes and bended knee.

More importantly is the yearning in the deepest hearts of woman and man, To set aside our desires and seek above all your plan.

Your fast includes not only the physical needs, But also the things on which our inner spirit feeds.

Sittin' on the Patio

*If the fast does not accomplish a change in the heart,
Then it was probably futile from the very start.*

*Your fast is meant to loose the bonds of wickedness,
And to bring us ultimately to a place of heartfelt repentance.*

The fast is to undo heavy burdens and let the oppressed go free, To break every yoke and let us be the people you want us to be.

The fast is to get our eyes off ourselves and onto others, Treating those we touch as truly sisters and brothers.

Then the light will break forth as in the morning; There will be no more frustration, worry or forlonging.

Our health shall spring forth quite suddenly indeed, And righteousness shall go before us as an incorruptible seed.

The glory of the Lord shall be completely all around, And the Lord will hear our call—a very precious sound.

The Lord will guide us and satisfy our souls. We will be like a spring as the cooling waters unfold.

As we delight in you, Lord, you cause us to rise to places high above, As you feed us with your grace, embracing us in your love.

So, Father, I hear what you are saying, and it is so very true. Minister your heart to me, and my love in turn will be manifested back to you.

Life Application:

God looks on our hearts and observes the motives in the things we do. What "He" sees is most important. Psalm 26:2-3 "Examine me, O Lord, and prove me; try my mind and my heart, for your lovingkindness is before my eyes, and I have walked in your truth."

Confession:

Father, the things that I do will be done as unto you, and to always bring you glory and joy.

DAY EIGHT

"But seek first the kingdom of God and his righteousness, and all these things shall be added to you."

—Matthew 6:33

*I'm sittin' on the patio with a cup of coffee in my hand,
Thanking God for this day and his great and glorious plan.*

Your Word on my lap opened to Philippians chapter four. Your Word is so rich, and its truths I always adore.

*Paul's love for his fellow-men was so strong and true
For he constantly encouraged them in the things they should do.*

And we can take his Words for them and apply them to you and to me, Enabling us to walk with Jesus, rejoicing and free.

Your Word declares to rejoice always, again and again. Your joy is our strength as we continue to stand.

You have said not to worry, but instead to give thanks in all things to you, And your peace, which is beyond understanding, will keep our hearts and minds fresh as

Sittin' on the Patio

dew.

You have said to be careful about the things to which our minds may resort, So that our thoughts be true, honest, just, pure, and lovely, and of good report.

You say to do all that which we learn, and that which we receive, And to be assured that we can do all things through Christ Jesus, in whom we believe.

You say to learn to be content in whatever state in which we may be, For then God's peace will surely abound and strengthen you and me.

All our needs you shall supply each day, According to your riches in glory by Jesus who made the way.

Father, I see that we each have a part to play, So that your peace comes into us to stay.

You have spoken, and now we must believe, receive, and do. It surely is simple when done in your strength, which enables us to be true.

Life Application:

God promises that if we put Him first and follow his Word, living in the spirit and trusting completely in Him, our lives will be so much better than we could ever have imagined. In Matthew 6:33, we read "But seek first the kingdom of God and his righteousness, and all these things shall be added to you."

Confession:

Father, today I give you first place in my life. Make me aware of those things that I need to push aside, for I know you will supply everything I need.

DAY NINE

"Looking unto Jesus, the author and finisher of our faith, who for the joy that was set before Him endured the cross, despising the shame, and has sat down at the right hand of the throne of God."

—Hebrews 12:2

I'm sittin' on the patio though the morning air is humid and hot, Realizing the magnitude of your creation, there is nothing you forgot.

Your Word opened to the first chapter of Colossians And the first verses I read were about your splendor in creation.

The Holy Spirit, through Paul, is talking about Jesus, your Son. You chose to dwell in Him in fullness as his work here on earth was done.

In Jesus, we have redemption, and we are delivered from the power of darkness. We are translated into his Kingdom of light in all its fullness.

Jesus was there at creation, accompanied by the Holy Spirit and God, too–Making things visible and invisible–all things brand new.

Jesus is the head of the body, the Church, by His blood,

Sittin' on the Patio

which He shed, On the cross for the redemption of man, so that rather than death we have life instead.

By accepting Jesus and walking in his glorious light We are presented to you, Holy, unblameable, and unreprovable in your sight.

We should desire to be filled with the knowledge of your will, So that in us all wisdom and spiritual understanding He will instill.

Therefore, we walk worthy of the Lord, pleasing Him in every way–Being fruitful in every good work and increasing in knowledge every day.

Praying that we might be strengthened with all might, And with joy we can then walk in patience, in longsuffering, and in light.

So let us give thanks to the One who has given us life To be partakers of His inheritance and to walk as saints in his light.

Father, today we see the great price you paid through your Son, And through accepting and following Him, we truly are one.

Life Application:

God has done his part through Jesus, our Lord and Savior. Now we must do our part in accepting all of His love and grace for the life He has given us. Hebrews 12:2 notes, "Looking unto Jesus, the author and finisher of our faith, who for the joy that was set before Him endured the cross, despising the shame, and has sat down at the right hand of the throne of God."

Confession:

I will abide with you as you abide with me, and I will enjoy your love and presence and power.

DAY TEN

"You will show me the path of life; in your presence is fullness of joy; at your right hand are pleasures forevermore."

—Psalm 16:11

I'm sittin' on the patio–it's early morning after a soaking summer rain. All that was parched and dry is refreshed, and green once again.

Your Word on my lap opened to Psalm thirty-four What do you have to reveal, Father, as your Word I explore?

Your desire is that we bless you and that we magnify your name, And receive and appropriate your promises–once said–still the same.

Your desire is that we taste and see just how good you are, As we trust that you are near–yes, not very far.

As we fear you, we are reassured all is supplied–no want indeed. As we seek you, we find all good things are supplied, and we are then freed.

It is certain that there are some things that we must do, Keeping our tongues from evil and our lips from guile, and seeking peace all the day through.

Sittin' on the Patio

Furthermore, the reward is so great–your part so blessed and wonderful; We know you hear us and deliver us out of all trouble.

Lord, we hear what you say as we do trust and obey You are faithful to provide and to protect all the way.

Life Application:

In this life, we have a part to play, as do you, Father. We find in Psalm 16:11, "You will show me the path of life; in your presence is fullness of joy; at your right hand are pleasures forevermore." What a marvelous deal we have!

Confession:

We will abide under the coverings of your wings as a hen covers her baby chicks; We will feel your warm assurance.

DAY ELEVEN

"Before I formed you in the womb, I knew you; before you were born, I sanctified you."

—Jeremiah 1:5

PAT STAHL

I'm sittin' on the patio just past the dawning of day Admiring the works of your creation, especially a tiny hummingbird at play.

This morning, Lord, I turned in your Word to Genesis chapter one–the creation of man. What is your Word for me today concerning your magnificent plan?

After five days of putting creation in place, You decided then to give your own spirit a face.

What a miracle indeed to make in your image a living spirit, Clothed with a body and containing a mind–so perfect in fit.

When you formed man from the dust of the earth, You breathed your life into him, giving him birth.

Just to think that inside man is the very breath of the God of creation. Of all of creation, no other being would have this special relation.

Sittin' on the Patio

In the beginning, there was no need for clothing, we know. Because man radiated your own shechinah glory from head to toe.

Man and woman had all they wanted or needed,

As long as God's commands they indeed heeded.

However, having a will to choose, they made a choice so wrong, Which will carry its consequences until time is ended–so very long.

Even though that miraculous relationship with God was broken by sin, You made a way by which it could be restored again.

You gave your Son Jesus to pay for the sins of mankind–what a cost, So that all could receive Him and none would be lost.

Today, Father, you are reaching out your loving and forgiving arms to restore; Man may repent of sin, and above all, your heart he would adore.

Life Application:

God has done quite a marvelous thing in creating us human beings. There is nothing that can in any way compare. He has entrusted us with the body He has given, so we can enjoy, nurture, and appreciate all that we are. Jeremiah 1:5 affirms, "Before I formed you in the womb, I knew you; before you were born, I sanctified you."

Confession:

I thank you for loving me enough to create me, nurture me, and sanctify me with your love and grace.

DAY TWELVE

"I am the way, the truth, and the life. No one comes to the Father except through me."

—John 14:6

I'm sittin' on the patio after the rain has cooled the summer day down, Thanking you for that favor, and so many others that freely abound.

I'm looking at your prayer for those who follow you What are you saying today, Lord, through your Word in Ephesians chapters one and two?

We can receive the spirit of wisdom and of revelation As we come to know you–to build that blessed relation.

The eyes of our understanding can become enlightened as well, To see the true meaning of your Word, as on it our minds dwell.

We can know the hope of your calling–your vision for us; We meditate upon the Word, and in it we learn to trust.

We can know and receive the riches of the glory of your inheritance, And the provisions you have made for us in

Sittin' on the Patio

every circumstance.

We can know the exceeding greatness of your power to those who believe, As the mighty works of your power in our lives, we receive.

We can have that same power in us that raised Jesus from the dead, For the Holy Spirit will dwell in our hearts, not in our heads.

As we live in Jesus and He lives in us each day, We can dwell in heavenly places and walk in heavenly ways.

In Christ, our position is with Him seated far above Constantly receiving his mighty power and wondrous love.

So, Lord, what are you showing me today? You are offering me a blessed life as I walk in your way.

A life of hope, provision, position, and power, Is just for the taking; it is mine at this very hour.

Life Application:

In Jesus, we have all the things we need or want to live out this abundant life. It is our choice to make Jesus the Lord and Savior of our lives and begin to live life to its fullest. Jesus states in John 14:6, "I am the way, the truth, and the life. No one comes to the Father except through me."

Confession:

I receive you, Jesus, and give myself totally to you.

DAY THIRTEEN

"My sheep hear my voice, and I know them, and they follow me."

—J<small>OHN</small> 10:27

I'm sittin' on the patio listening to the early morning sounds, Realizing and enjoying your presence and your goodness that truly abounds.

This morning, as I opened your Word, Psalm twenty-three came to mind. What do you have to reveal to me, and what new treasures can I find?

You are my shepherd watching over me and keeping me safe from the enemy's taunt. You are saving me and providing for me–no reason to want.

My heart's desire is to fellowship with you as you lead me to stop and look up. You quench my thirst and overflow my cup.

My mind is renewed and restored by your presence and your Word; Your voice leads me to a right relationship by peace, not by sword.

Though I have to face destruction and even death in

Sittin' on the Patio

this life, You are with me to protect and comfort–no need for fear or for strife.

Though enemies may be all around, your table of provision is there. Your healing is mine with abundantly more blessings to spare.

Your goodness and your mercy will never run out And I can stay with you now and forever–that deserves a shout!

So Lord, what are you speaking to me today that I should heed? You are El Shaddai–more than enough– meeting my every need.

So many promises are found all through your Word And I thank you for the ones on this day that I have seen and have heard.

Life Application:

God has provided His love as our great Shepherd–one who always looks after His sheep. He keeps us close to Himself and offers us all things we need as we acknowledge Him and receive Him. Jesus confirms in John 10:27, "My sheep hear my voice, and I know them, and they follow me."

Confession:

Father, I know your voice; I will always follow you.

DAY FOURTEEN

"You have turned for me my mourning into dancing You have put off my sackcloth and clothed me with gladness, To the end that my glory may sing praise to You and not be silent. O Lord my God, I will give thanks to You forever."

—Psalm 30:11-12

I'm sittin' on the patio listening to the squawking of a crow and the cooing of a dove; Each reminds me how opposite the world and the spirit–so choose the way of love.

I'm reading in Isaiah chapter fifty-one about mourning and joy–opposites for certain. What do you want to teach me? My heart is waiting for you to draw back the curtain.

Your Word promises you will turn our mourning into dancing. This can be ours anytime, just for the asking.

The spirit of fear and sadness does not originate with you; It is from the enemy to try to prevent us from living a life free, abundant, and true.

Those whom you redeemed and saved from the world to your church, Shall come with much joy and singing as they complete their long search.

Sittin' on the Patio

What the world offered was sorrow and mourning. You have replaced those with gladness and joy–our hearts adorning.

When a loved one dies, fear and loneliness try to attach themselves to us, But you are our peace and comfort and always with us–if we but trust.

How can we ever forget you, Lord, who made the earth and man? How you laid the heavens in place as you stretched forth your hand?

Your Word says that no matter what sadness this life may bring, Knowing we are your chosen gives us hope and makes us sing.

As we walk through the dark times of life,

Assurance of your presence can be ours–no need for strife.

Life Application:

Because we live in a fallen world, we will face times in our lives that bring us grief and confusion. As we turn to you in those times, the blood of Jesus has been shed abroad in our hearts. We can thank and praise you for your comfort and strength. Psalm 107:2 encourages us, "Let the redeemed of the Lord say so!"

Confession:

We praise you for redeeming us from the power of satan and filling us with the power of your Holy Spirit. We will praise you with joy; we will choose happiness.

DAY FIFTEEN

"*Behold, children are a heritage from the Lord, The fruit of the womb is a reward. Like arrows in the hand of a warrior, So are the children of one's youth Happy is the man who has his quiver full of them They shall not be ashamed, But shall speak with their enemies in the gate.*"

—Psalm 127:3-5

I'm sittin' on another patio in a different place; my Bible with me I did take. I'm looking out at the sun glistening and making sparkles on the lake;

It's so powerful–like a bit of Heaven it appears Today, what do you have to say to my heart and my spiritual ears?

Psalm 127 talks about children and how precious they are to you, Lord, They are a part of your plan and to you a great reward.

They are like arrows placed in a quiver in the hand of man, Who is given the responsibility to point them in the best direction to which they will land.

Sometimes the arrow placed in the bow has to be pulled so tightly! Discipline and correction with love can make a child's life perform so rightly.

Children bring happiness to their parents in so many

SITTIN' ON THE PATIO

ways, As they honor their parents, they can even lengthen their very own days.

Though God has no grandchildren--only children, of course, We grandparents on earth are blessed to be their source,

Of wisdom and guidance through God's direction Which helps to nudge them onto their road of perfection.

So happy is the man and woman who have many children or just one. Especially when they see the child or children accept Jesus for their salvation, He won.

Hence, what are you saying, Lord, that I should see Children are a treasure to love and to draw very near to me.

Life Application:

There are few greater blessings than children. They keep our hearts young and give us opportunities to nurture them with God's love and with his Word. Even if a married couple doesn't have children of their own, God can direct them to reach out to some child in need of their love and God's love. Mark 9:37 affirms, "Whoever receives one of these little children in my name receives me."

Confession:

We thank you, Lord, for children and the role they play in your great plan of life.

DAY SIXTEEN

> "Now may the God of hope fill you with all joy and peace in believing, that you may abound in hope by the power of the Holy Spirit."
>
> —Romans 15:13

I'm sitting on the patio listening to the early morning sounds from the lake, Looking at nature's wonders and the many miraculous things you did make.

What do you have to say to me through the beauty of the sunrise? What can I hear with my spiritual ears and see with my spiritual eyes?

As in Philippians chapter four, to think of you makes me rejoice. When I spend time with you, it is the very best choice.

Your Word says not to worry about anything at all But in all things to give thanks to you and on your name to call.

Your peace goes beyond all we can ever imagine or think. Praying to you and believing is that trustworthy link.

It is so important to think on the things that bring you

Sittin' on the Patio

praise. Our thoughts must be guarded for all of our days.

Things that are true, honest, just, pure, lovely, and good, Are virtuous and for the heart, really good food.

So, Lord, in the midst of all you have so generously given, Trusting in you is truly a life worth living.

Life Application:

God has given us all things that we need to live this life on earth, so let us give back to Him our love and our trust. Romans 15:13 says, "Now may the God of hope fill you with all joy and peace in believing, that you may abound in hope by the power of the Holy Spirit."

Confession:

Father, I will trust you and love you with all my heart and I am thankful for all you are and for all you do.

DAY SEVENTEEN

"When He, the Spirit of truth, has come, He will guide you into all truth; for He will not speak on his own authority; but whatever He hears He will speak, and He will tell you things to come."

— JOHN 16:13

I'm sittin' on the patio watching a bird attack my cat, which has gotten near her nest. What a wonder of God– a tiny bird against a large cat–what zest!

That reminds me of our stand against the devil, And how the playing field is not at all level.

For you have already won the victory against the evil one, When your blood was shed on Calvary, the deal was indeed done.

Your Word in 1 Peter 5:8-9 about our adversary comes to mind; We see his evil tactics and the help we can find.

You tell us to be sober and to be clear-minded Vigilant, and ever on guard so as not to be blinded.

Why? Because our adversary is always walking around, Searching for any unwary victim to be found.

Sittin' on the Patio

*He walks as a roaring lion, though he is not one at all,
But he wants to instill fear and cause us to fall.*

However, if we are not watchful every moment of every hour, He has the potential to surely snare us and our hopes to devour.

We must not only watch but we must also resist his deception, Making certain not to give him even the slightest reception.

We need to stand firm in our faith with complete trust, That Jesus has already completely won the battle for us.

The devil will be up to his tricks as long as on this earth we live, But our victory is found when to God our devotion we give.

So, Lord, you are assuring us to stand firmly today with You, And whatever Satan brings our way, you will see us through.

Life Application:

We live in a fallen world where Satan is the "God" of our world. His lease will end very soon when Jesus returns, but until then, we need to keep our eyes on Jesus and trust the Holy Spirit for guidance and protection. John 16:13 says, "When He, the Spirit of truth, has come, He will guide you into all truth; for He will not speak on his own authority; but whatever He hears He will speak, and He will tell you things to come."

Confession:

Father, thank you for the Holy Spirit who lives within to guide us into all truth and to keep us from fear of the enemy.

DAY EIGHTEEN

"All scripture is given by God, and is profitable for doctrine, for reproof, for correction, for instruction in righteousness, that the man of God may be complete, thoroughly equipped for every good work."

—2 Timothy 3:16-17

I'm sittin' on the patio listening to a dog barking to the top of her voice. Will I ignore it, or will I let it distract me? Refusing to listen to it will be my choice.

For I look above to the beautiful blue sky laced with clouds, pink and gold, And think of the wonders and blessings of God–so many yet to unfold.

Your Word in Proverbs chapter six speaks much about those who choose to sleep, About those who are lazy, and those who allow the jaws of poverty to run deep.

Just what can I learn from you today, Lord, as on your Word I meditate? What Words can I hear as in your voice and presence I wait?

Your Word says to go to the ant and consider her ways and be wise. She is always working and productive, though so small in size.

She doesn't have an overseer or even a guide, But she

knows what to do from on the inside.

She provides her meat in the summer and gathers food in the harvest, Thus, when winter weather comes, she will have stored the very best.

How like her we should be in our Christian walk Using God's wisdom as we work and as we talk.

We, too, as compared with all of creation, are quite small in size, But indwelled with God's Spirit as born-again believers, we can be wise.

Like the ant, we can find our direction from deep inside, Through your Holy Spirit, who is our constant guide.

Your spirit gives us wisdom to know how to provide for our own, And the heart to help others when the need is made known.

Like the ant, we are to help each other, working side by side, To accomplish God's desire that all will come to Him to abide.

So, Lord, you are telling us in your Word as you say To put away laziness and to take on diligence every day.

*We are to lean on your wisdom in all that we do,
Receive your guidance, and stay in your presence, too.*

Life Application:

We must work for our physical sustenance as well as for our spiritual growth. 2 Thess. 3:10 states, "If anyone will not work, neither shall he eat." And 2 Timothy 3:16-17 reads, "All scripture is given by God, and is profitable for doctrine, for reproof, for correction, for instruction in righteousness, that the man of God may be complete, thoroughly equipped for every good work."

Confession:

Father, we will be diligent in our work both for our physical needs and for our spiritual needs.

DAY NINETEEN

> "If any of you lacks wisdom, let him ask of God, who gives to all liberally, and without reproach, and it will be given to him."
>
> —James 1:5

I'm sittin' on the patio at the beginning of another hot, summer day, Spending time with you, Lord, and listening to what you have to say.

The scripture came to me in 1 Cor. 1:17-31 about how God, in his wisdom, Used the foolish things of this world to bring the wise to confusion.

It seems that God and the world are on two different tracks of thought, And when we go the world's way, many times our destination comes to nought.

For God chose the things of the world which are weak, To confound the things which are mighty–God alone mankind must seek.

Some of the miracle healings Jesus did seemed unusual, but they made things better, For Jesus always heard from his Father, following his direction to the letter.

The foolish things of God are wiser than those of man,

Sittin' on the Patio

And the weakness of God is stronger than man's strength can withstand.

God chose the base things of the world, which are despised, And brought to nothing the higher things that man surmised.

God is a loving, but jealous God indeed, Wanting all the glory for Jesus, his seed.

He knows in his wisdom if man glories in his flesh Pride will be exalted, and the end result is not more, but less.

So, Lord, you seem to be indicating in these contrasting situations, For mankind to trust in you and to wait for your directions and revelations.

Life Application:

During our lives, we are free to choose the way of God or the way of the world. In James 1:5, we find our direction: "If any of you lacks wisdom, let him ask of God, who gives to all liberally, and without reproach, and it will be given to him."

Confession:

I will choose your way, Lord, knowing that you go before me and prepare the way.

DAY TWENTY

"And the Word became flesh and dwelt among us, and we beheld His glory, the glory as of the only begotten of the Father, full of grace and truth."

—John 1:14

I'm sittin' on the patio listening to a dove cooing in the distance. I'm realizing the peace that comes from staying in your presence.

Sitting on my lap is your Word–a powerhouse indeed, So satisfying and fulfilling as on it I continually feed.

John 1:1-18 comes to mind, relating to us that Jesus was the Word made flesh. He took on the body of a man, giving us a chance with Him to mesh.

Jesus, with God and the Holy Spirit, made all things in the beginning of time, But He gave up his heavenly position to redeem fallen mankind.

When He was in the world, the world didn't know who He was; Even his own people rejected Him as well as his cause.

He was sent by God in the midst of darkness as a light to man, So that any who would receive Him would be saved and not fall, but stand.

To those who did receive Him, He gave them eternal life; He made them sons of God—so very simple, no strife.

He freed man from the impossible keeping of the law given by Moses, For "In Him" the law was fulfilled through grace—sweeter than roses.

So today, Lord, we thank you for Jesus, your Son, the light, And we receive Him as Lord and Savior, choosing to do what is right.

No one has ever seen God, except God's only Son, But Jesus is at God's side so that to us God can be known.

Life Application:

For God to let his only begotten Son give up his Heavenly position to become flesh and to dwell among us is the ultimate gift. Our hearts are full of love and gratitude for this everlasting gift. Romans 6:23 tells us, "For the wages of sin is death, but the gift of God is eternal life in Christ Jesus our Lord."

Confession:

We choose life this day through the only one who has made possible the path for us.

DAY TWENTY ONE

"And we know that all things work together for good to those who love God, to those who are called according to his purpose."

—Romans 8:28

I'm sittin' on the patio with the fan gently stirring the summer air, Thinking about your many blessings and of my privilege to share.

Your Word in 1 Timothy 4:14-16 comes to mind, where you said, "To stir up the gift that is within and do not leave it as dead."

As born-again believers, you gave us a new spirit within, To fellowship with you and to lead a life not controlled by sin.

What a treasure inside our bodies does abide; How sad to ever let the ability of that treasure subside.

Just as embers need to be stirred to increase its own fire, So your Holy Spirit needs to be stirred to fulfill your desire.

By meditating on your Word and by worshipping you each day, That gift that is within is rekindled and

Sittin' on the Patio

ablaze; it will stay.

As we are diligent in walking in the gifts you have generously given, We give ourselves wholly as we are Holy Spirit driven.

Not only will an individual, but also others as well, surely benefit, From this gift and its use and release among those with whom we may sit.

As we live our lives and follow the doctrine you have put before us, We persevere to save others and, through our gifts, win their trust.

So, Father, today, we see that you have indeed blessed each of us, As we stir up your gift and walk it out in your complete trust.

Life Application:

Each of us has a specific purpose in his or her walk with the Lord. As we use the gifts God has given us, we can unite with each other to bring his love and power to those around us–becoming true brothers and sisters in the family of God. In Romans 8:28, we find these words, "And we know that all things work together for good to those who love God, to those who are called according to his purpose."

Confession:

We will walk in the spirit and be thankful in all things that we may be a light to the world.

DAY TWENTY TWO

> "*...and it shall come to pass in the last days, says God, that I will pour out my Spirit on all flesh; your sons and your daughters shall prophesy, your young men shall see visions, your old men shall dream dreams.*"
>
> —Acts 2:17

I'm sittin' on the patio; the air is cooler out here than the air inside. Our air conditioner has leaked out its ability the cooling to provide.

This situation reminds me of the many scriptures in Acts where men with the Holy Spirit were filled, But then later on, needed more filling as if some of the spirit had spilled.

To remain faithful to the world while trying to walk with God each day, Is like the continual pouring of Freon into an air conditioner while letting the leak still stay.

As we come into obedience to God and leave the world behind, Our spirit will stay filled as God's many promises in his Word we find.

Just as Acts 2:4, where the one hundred and twenty were filled with the Holy Spirit, Our continual visitation with God will keep our spirit lit.

Sittin' on the Patio

Today, Lord, you are telling us that we need to stay near, To continually feed our spirit to do your will with no reason to fear.

Life Application:

In this world, much of you is needed, Lord. We need more of your spirit, more of your grace, more of your love, and more of your guidance. Thank you for making your Holy Spirit available to us, enabling us to receive all of you. In Acts 2:17, one reads about God through these abbreviated words from the prophet Joel: "and it shall come to pass in the last days, says God, that I will pour out my Spirit on all flesh; your sons and your daughters shall prophesy, your young men shall see visions, your old men shall dream dreams."

Confession:

We believe and receive your Holy Spirit into our hearts to remain with us until our lives are completed on this earth.

DAY TWENTY THREE

"Brethren, I do not count myself to have apprehended; but one thing I do, forgetting those things which are behind and reaching forward to those things which are ahead, I press toward the goal for the prize of the upward call of God in Christ Jesus."

—P<small>HILLIPIANS</small> 3:13-14

I'm sittin' on the patio; the day is already humid and warm. However, this is a new day with many opportunities to love and not harm.

Phillipians 3:13-14 comes to mind, encouraging us to forget the past and to look ahead. Today is what you give us, and through it we must be led.

In this message from Paul regarding perfection, he has not yet gained. However, there are some things he absolutely has attained.

We are to forget those things which are behind–failures and the like, Which Satan uses to bring us down; we need to tell him "to take a hike"!

We must reach forth to the things which are yet to come to us, Keeping our eyes on Jesus, He blesses all our trust.

With our hearts outstretched, we need to really press on

Sittin' on the Patio

with all we are, And fight the good fight of faith as if in a real war.

The goal is there before us; the prize is worth it all Get up and keep on running, even though many times we may fall.

So, Lord, we thank you that as our race is won,

You are there to receive us and to say to us, "Well done."

Life Application:

In the here and now, we are definitely in a race. If our lives have been given to God and we have received Jesus, his Son, as our Savior and Lord, we have all we need for the race. As in life, there will be times when we stumble and fall, but with God's grace, we pick ourselves up and keep on running. Psalm 145:14 says, "The Lord upholds all who fall, and raises up all who are bowed down."

Confession:

We prepare ourselves to run our race through your Word, prayer, and praise. We then set our face toward the prize of the high calling of Christ Jesus.

DAY TWENTY FOUR

"Finally, brethren, whatever things are true, whatever things are noble, whatever things are just, whatever things are pure, whatever things are lovely, whatever things are of good report, if there is any virtue and if there is anything praiseworthy— meditate on these things."

—Phillipians 4:8

*I'm sittin' on the patio just as dawn is finally breaking.
The peacefulness and wonder of the new day is breathtaking.*

*Lord, you are first and foremost in our thoughts today,
And you are the fulfillment of your Word in Phillipians 4:8 in every way.*

You tell us in your Word what kind of things should fill our minds, Things that are true, honest, just, pure, and lovely, and of good report–those kinds.

Your Word is truth, and Jesus, the Word, has the power to set us free, For He lived an honest life, putting to shame those who would cheat others, you see.

He was just giving his life for all who will believe, He was pure, never sinning, that we, his believers, might receive.

He is more lovely than any worldly thing can display.

Sittin' on the Patio

His Word is filled with good reports for our meditation each day.

As we think on things, let us hold them up to the light of the Word–each one indeed. Consider if they are worth thinking on to produce blessed seed.

Jesus, you care what our minds meditate on each day; Let us guard our minds, allowing only things of God to stay.

Life Application:

It is our choice as to what things we choose to think on. We need to choose only those things that make our lives better, not on those things that pull us down. Our minds are a wonderful gift. Phillipians 4:7 declares, "And the peace of God, which surpasses all understanding, will guard your hearts and minds through Christ Jesus."

Confession:

We thank you, Lord, for guarding our minds and for leading us in righteousness.

DAY TWENTY FIVE

"When the day of Pentecost had fully come, they were all with one accord in one place. And suddenly there came a sound from heaven, as of a rushing mighty wind, and it filled the whole house where they were sitting. Then there appeared to them divided tongues, as of fire, and one sat upon each one of them. And they were all filled with the Holy Spirit and began to speak with other tongues, as the Spirit gave them utterance."

—Acts 2:1-4

*I'm sittin' on the patio; the hour is early in the morning.
As the day is beginning, things are quickly forming.*

*The grass is fresh and green, wet with the morning dew.
The pears are clutched on the tree–more than just a
few.*

*It's so peaceful and still; sounds abound, including the
birds' singing. What blessings on this day could you be
bringing?*

*What would you like for us to think on today? What
special Word of faith will be on our tongues to stay?*

*John 14:16-19 tells us about the Holy Spirit within He
is our comforter, guide, teacher, and friend.*

*Your Word, Jesus, says you pray to the Father for
believers; we see. When you returned to your Father,
you sent your Holy Spirit within us to be.*

Sittin' on the Patio

*He will live within us every moment of every day,
Teaching us about your love and guiding us on life's way.*

The world cannot receive Him because He is never seen, Nor can they know Him or upon his wisdom lean.

As born-again believers, that is not the case with us. We know Him, and by faith, His indwelt presence we can trust.

The Holy Spirit always teaches us and glorifies you, Jesus, And helps us in our faith walk, as on Him we daily trust.

He is right inside this body of flesh and bone, The actual Spirit of God living in us; it is His home.

How blessed we are to have this great Spirit within Knowing Him, fellowshipping with Him, and calling Him our special friend.

He is gentle and humble–never forcing Himself on us; He is always available when we seek his guidance in which we trust.

So, Father, we thank you for your great wisdom and love, And for sending us a part of you, your Holy Spirit from above.

Thank you, Jesus, for providing salvation and deliverance on the cross, So that we can experience all of the God–head and never be lost.

This morning, we hear you saying through your Word so clearly, so plain, Get more closely acquainted with your Holy Spirit, for He always lifts up your name.

Yes, we know the Holy Spirit; He is here in our hearts. We are open to all the wisdom and love that He will impart.

So thank you, Father, for yourself, Jesus, the Holy Spirit, and your Word, And especially your voice in our hearts that can really be heard.

Thank you for being a good and gracious Father of love; Blessing us with your spirit and pointing us to wonders above.

As we meet with the Holy Spirit, we thank you each day, Drawing closer to Him in an ever-growing way.

Sittin' on the Patio

Life Application:

We are taught about God and Jesus, but we also need to know about the Holy Spirit. The early disciples knew God, and they also knew Jesus. However, they had to wait on the promise of the Holy Spirit. Acts 2:1-4 teaches us, "When the day of Pentecost had fully come, they were all with one accord in one place. And suddenly there came a sound from heaven, as of a rushing mighty wind, and it filled the whole house where they were sitting. Then there appeared to them divided tongues, as of fire, and one sat upon each one of them. And they were all filled with the Holy Spirit and began to speak with other tongues, as the Spirit gave them utterance."

Confession:

Lord, we want all of you, including the abundant presence of the Holy Spirit.

DAY TWENTY SIX

"Let the words of my mouth and the meditation of my heart be acceptable in your sight, O Lord, my strength and my redeemer."

—Psalm 19:14

*I'm sittin' on the patio watching the rain pouring down,
As if heaven itself opened up to water the dry and thirsty ground.*

The rain makes us think of Noah and the great flood in his days of old, So we turned in your Word to Genesis chapters six through nine to see what we are told.

Before Noah, there had never been rain on the earth. How crazy people thought Noah was to build the great Ark—of what worth?

However, Noah had heard from God as to just what to do, So he and his three sons persisted until it was all through.

The day finally came when God told Noah and his family to enter the Ark. The time had come for them, along with two of every living creature, on a cruise to embark.

Sittin' on the Patio

After all were safely inside, God shut the door. Soon, all the unrighteous would perish; they would be no more.

For forty days God poured rain on the earth, covering every living thing, But for Noah, his family, and the living creatures God would safely them bring.

When at last the waters had receded, Noah walked on dry ground. God placed a rainbow in the sky, a new covenant with Him was bound.

He promised to never destroy the earth with water— never again. He used Noah and his family and the living creatures to increase life again.

Now these many centuries later, when we see the rainbow in the sky, We are assured that God's promise will never be outdated nor ever die.

Father, we see that Noah took you at your Word, Putting actions with his faith in your directions, which he heard.

However, you are reminding us in this very century as well, To be not only hearers but also doers of your Word—it will never fail.

Thank you for that beautiful rainbow we often see in the sky, Reminding us of Noah's faith, as many days have gone by.

May it encourage us in our walk of faith with you,

And as we listen to your voice, guiding us in every day that is new.

Life Application:

God's Word is filled with his promises, and we can count on each of them. As we read your promises and apply them to our lives, we are continually encouraged to meditate on your Word. In Psalm 19:14, we read, "Let the words of my mouth and the meditation of my heart be acceptable in your sight, O Lord, my strength and my redeemer."

Confession:

We will be faithful to keep your Word always before us and trust in it with all our hearts, speaking it in faith.

DAY TWENTY SEVEN

> *"For our light affliction, which is but for a moment, is working for us a far more exceeding and eternal glory, while we do not look at the things which are seen, but at the things that are not seen. For the things which are seen are temporary, but the things which are not seen are eternal."*
>
> —2 Corinthians 4:17-18

I'm sittin' on the patio listening to the songs of a mockingbird, Chirping his several songs loudly enough to surely be heard.

In the early morning hours, all is calm and serene, As this day holds many things in which you have opportunity to intervene.

My Bible is open to Acts chapter five, where the apostles were being threatened on every side. What do you want to impart to us today, Father, as in your Word we abide?

When things are breaking loose all around us, It is in you that we must ultimately trust.

For you alone see the big picture, entire and complete; Whereas, we can see only what is at hand and get into defeat.

When the apostles were threatened of death, their eyes

Sittin' on the Patio

focused on you. Their thoughts were of others they could take their message to.

They prayed to you, Father, to grant unto them power and boldness, So that in that threatening hour, they could continue to be your witness.

Your answer came; the place where they assembled was shaken. They had prayed, and in you their trust had been taken.

They began to witness of your own resurrection with great power, The power that was needful to win the lost in that very hour.

Not only did they receive your grace to speak for you, But also upon them great grace you did endue.

Father, we hear what you are declaring through your Word; By trusting in you for power and boldness, your message will be heard.

By trusting you in the midst of turmoil in a place, You will provide what we need, not only grace, but also great grace.

Life Application:

In this life, we will face times of turmoil and even threats. Our trust in you will be strengthened as we walk through those times without fear. 2 Corinthians 4:17-18 affirms, "For our light affliction, which is but for a moment, is working for us a far more exceeding and eternal glory, while we do not look at the things which are seen, but at the things that are not seen. For the things which are seen are temporary, but the things which are not seen are eternal."

Confession:

No matter what may come our way, we are assured that you will never leave us nor forsake us.

DAY TWENTY EIGHT

"So Jesus answered and said to them, "Have faith in God. For assuredly, I say to you, whoever says to this mountain, 'Be removed and be cast into the sea,' and does not doubt in his heart, but believes that those things he says will be done, he will have whatever he says. Therefore I say to you, whatever things you ask when you pray, believe that you receive them, and you will have them."

—Mark 11:22-24

I'm sittin' on the patio at the beginning of September, Labor Day. I'm thinking of the many opportunities of life God provides along the way.

1 Thessalonians 4:11-12 tells us to provide with the work of our own hand, That we may reap and eat of the plenty of the land.

In Matthew 6:33, we are told to seek God's kingdom first, And all things will be added to us; we will never hunger nor thirst.

Therefore, how do the promises of the heavenly realm, Become a reality in this physical world in which we dwell?

Just the same way as God did when He created the world, He spoke the Word, and creation began to unfurl.

In Mark 11:23, Jesus says three times to "say" what

Sittin' on the Patio

you believe, And then those things spoken, you will indeed receive.

As we go to the Word of God and find what is written therein, We can begin to speak His promises and see new things begin.

Thank you, Father, for your will bestowed to me through Jesus' blood, And thank you for the promise that many blessings to my life will bring good.

Life Application:

When God created the world, He "spoke" and it became. This is our example to follow in our daily Christian walk. We must believe and then speak God's Word. Mark 11:24 declares, "Therefore I say to you, whatever things you ask when you pray, believe that you receive them and you will have them." Be bold and speak forth the Word of God.

Confession:

Father, today we will search your Word. We believe what it says, and we will speak forth our confession.

DAY TWENTY NINE

"*Having your conduct honorable among the Gentiles, that, when they speak against you as evildoers, they may, by your good works which they observe, glorify God in the day of visitation.*"

—1 Peter 2:12

I'm sittin' on the patio enjoying the presence of God–so sweet. The rain is gently falling–what an early morning treat.

I'm reading in Deut. 28:1-13 about God's blessings so very plentiful, To those who diligently hearken to his voice, and to those who of His Word become mindful.

How can we hearken to your voice? We can grasp it in several ways. One is to keep our thoughts on you throughout all of our days.

Another is that we can pray in the spirit and listen for your interpretation. We know you want to be a part of every activity–every occasion.

We can also pray in English as well and listen as you speak, The answers to the spoken prayers; yes, your answers we do seek.

Furthermore, we can meditate on your written Word,

Sittin' on the Patio

spiritually eating it like meat, Thinking about it, studying it, speaking it over and over–repeat, repeat.

We can keep our whole being alert to your intervention in our lives, Through a change of plan or direction to help us avoid useless drives.

Father, today we thank you for who you are and for your great love. You love mankind so much that you gave your only Son from above.

Thank you for the great price Jesus paid on the cross, So that anyone who would believe in Him will never be lost.

Thank you for creating man so that he could communicate with you, In word, in action, in preaching, and in teaching, just to name a few.

Life Application:

The blessings of God are great in number and in might. Let us use those blessings in the best ways we can so that they are never wasted, but always glorify our precious Father.

1 Peter 2:12 says, "Having your conduct honorable among the Gentiles, that, when they speak against you as evildoers, they may, by your good works which they observe, glorify God in the day of visitation."

Confession:

Let my whole life be a blessing to you in all that I do and say.

DAY THIRTY

"This Book of the Law shall not depart from your mouth, but you shall meditate in it day and night, that you may observe to do according to all that is written in it. For then you will make your way prosperous, and then you will have good success. Have I not commanded you? Be strong and of good courage; do not be afraid, nor be dismayed, for the Lord your God is with you wherever you go."

—Joshua 1:8-9

I'm sittin' on the patio thinking about the riches of God's Word as I read, Realizing how much more wisdom, knowledge, and understanding I need.

So Father, as I contemplate, think on, dwell on your Word to me, Give me revelation that your truths be not hidden, but that I may see.

In Joshua 1:5-9, you have promised to be with us as you were with Moses, Even until our time on earth closes.

You also tell us to meditate on your Word day and night, So that which you command us can be completed with great might.

You promise, as we put your Word first, that we will prosper and succeed; In fact, all things will be added to us, indeed.

We love your Word and we honor and worship you,

Sittin' on the Patio

Fully acknowledging all your promises to be true.

Thank you for your Word and for Jesus–the Word made flesh. Thank you for the Holy Spirit and His help to make all things rightly mesh.

Today, we stand on your Word and do count it as a fact, That as you were with Moses, we, too, will have no lack.

Life Application:

Whatever we may need in this life, God is our source. We find in Phillipains 4:19 these words, "And my God shall supply all your needs according to his riches in glory by Christ Jesus."

Confession:

We thank you, Father, for loving us and for providing for us. We thank you, too, for accepting our adoration and praise of you.

DAY THIRTY ONE

"The thief does not come except to steal, and to kill, and to destroy. I have come that they may have life, and that they may have it more abundantly."

—John 10:10

I'm sittin' on the patio enjoying the briskness of the morning air. Although it is hot summer, God has sent a cool, gentle breeze to share.

You are such a giving God, always supplying our every need. What Word do you have for us today? What teaching should we heed?

In Luke 6:38, you teach us how to give unto you through others, Thus, our own needs may be met by them or by other brothers.

You say to give a good measure—more, not less, If we want to receive your abundance with which you bless.

You say to shake it down and to press it together, too. So as to give all that can be given, and running over before we are through.

You will cause men to give to us what we need, As you prick their hearts toward the multiplying of our seed.

Sittin' on the Patio

*In actual measure and in the attitude of a giving heart,
We can expect your abundant return to impart.*

*You are saying that a basic life principle is that of
giving, To receive and enjoy an abundance of living.*

Life Application:

God cannot bless us if we approach Him with a closed fist. But if we come to Him with open hands and an open heart, He is able to do for us more than we can ever expect. John 10:10 says,

"The thief does not come except to steal, and to kill, and to destroy. I have come that they may have life, and that they may have it more abundantly."

Confession:

We will give to you of our worldly possessions and expect to receive from you all that we may need or even more.

ABOUT THE AUTHOR

As the only child of Percy and Hazel Mullins, I was born on December 4, 1940, in the Minden Hospital and was given the name, Patricia Ann Mullins. Until I began school, I lived with my grandparents, Fred and Minnie Gruner, while my parents worked. At 5 1/2 years of age, I entered elementary school, which was just across the street from our home. All my school years were in Minden, and I graduated from Minden High School in 1958 as Salutatorian. My next venture was Spencer-Draughan Business College. After his graduation, also as Salutatorian, on June 7, 1959, the love of my life, Harry Doyce Stahl, and I were married. After my mother died in 1960, we bought the home from my dad and lived there on Elm Street. Harry worked in finance, and I in secretarial.

Our two boys were born; Douglas Wayne in 1962 and David Layne in 1965. After their completion of school in Minden, they both married. In the following years, 8 grandchildren were born, as well as 7 great-grandchildren. In 1999, we moved across town to a home where we could entertain, which we enjoyed for several years. We joined Living Word Church in 1999 and became active members. Harry went to be with the Lord in 2017. My granddaughter, Aubrie, has lived with me in my home for 2 years and is a comfort and a blessing. I still teach the Adult Sunday School class at Living Word and lead a life-group in my home twice each month. God has been so good to me, and I am thankful.

www.ingramcontent.com/pod-product-compliance
Lightning Source LLC
Chambersburg PA
CBHW070100080526
44586CB00013B/1131